# What do you
## honey

There are three types of honeybees. Queen bees lay eggs.

queen

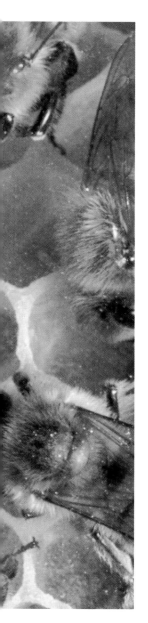

Male bees, called drones, mate with the queen. Small female bees, called workers, do many jobs.

drone

worker

All honeybees live in large groups called colonies.

Each colony lives in its own hive in a tree or log.

The worker bees in each colony use the wax their bodies make to build a honeycomb.

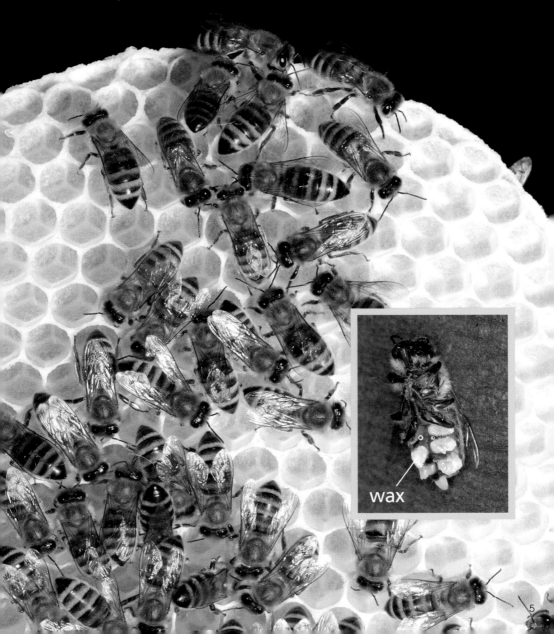

wax

Workers sometimes hang together in a chain to build the honeycomb cells.

After the honeycomb is built, the queen bee lays up to 1,500 eggs a day, each in a different honeycomb cell.

The eggs hatch into wormlike larvae. It's the worker bees' job to feed the larvae until they grow into pupae.

The developing pupae now grow eyes, legs, and wings.

When a bee is fully grown, it pushes itself out of the cell and joins the other bees in the colony.

Another job worker bees do is collect a yellow dust called pollen from the inside of flowers.

They brush the pollen that collects all over their bodies into the pollen baskets on their back legs.

pollen basket

Back at the hive, they store it in cells to be fed to baby bees.

Worker bees also sip nectar from flowers.

Then they spread the nectar in the honeycomb cells to make honey.

Worker guard bees protect the honey
and other bees from outsiders.

But sometimes . . .

even the busiest of bees needs to rest.